midweek meals

THE AUSTRALIAN Women's Weekly

CONTENTS

AUSTRALIAN CUP AND SPOON MEASUREMENTS ARE METRIC. A CONVERSION CHART APPEARS ON PAGE 77.

When we get home from work, the last thing we want is to spend hours in the kitchen cooking up dinner. Fast and simple, that's what we need, and that's what this great little book is all about...food that's not just ready in a flash, but also tastes good. There's even a selection of 15-minute dishes, for those days when you need to dash right back out again.

Pamela Clark

Food Director

CHILLI, SALT AND PEPPER SEAFOOD STIR-FRY

prep & cook time 30 minutes **serves** 4
nutritional count per serving 11g total fat (2.2g saturated fat); 1070kJ (256 cal); 2.7g carbohydrate; 35.8g protein; 1.2g fibre

500g uncooked medium king prawns
300g cleaned squid hoods
300g scallops, roe removed
2 teaspoons sea salt
½ teaspoon cracked black pepper
½ teaspoon five-spice powder
2 fresh small red thai chillies, chopped finely
2 tablespoons peanut oil
150g sugar snap peas, trimmed
2 tablespoons light soy sauce
1 lime, cut into wedges

1 Shell and devein prawns, leaving tails intact. Cut squid down centre to open out; score inside in diagonal pattern then cut into thick strips.
2 Combine seafood, salt, pepper, five-spice and chilli in large bowl.
3 Heat half the oil in wok; stir-fry seafood, in batches, until cooked. Remove from wok.
4 Heat remaining oil in wok; stir-fry peas until tender. Return seafood to wok with sauce; stir-fry until hot. Serve seafood with lime.

SEAFOOD

salmon steaks with tarragon sauce and grilled asparagus

SALMON STEAKS WITH TARRAGON SAUCE AND GRILLED ASPARAGUS

prep & cook time **35 minutes** serves **4**
nutritional count per serving **51g total fat (27.3g saturated fat); 3281kJ (785 cal); 27g carbohydrate; 48g protein; 4.9g fibre**

4 medium potatoes (800g), sliced thickly
500g asparagus, trimmed
4 x 200g salmon fillets
tarragon sauce
20g butter
1 medium brown onion (150g), chopped finely
½ cup (125ml) dry white wine
300ml cream
2 tablespoons finely chopped fresh tarragon

1 Make tarragon sauce.
2 Meanwhile, boil, steam or microwave potato until just tender; drain.
3 Cook potato, asparagus and fish on heated oiled grill plate, uncovered, until potato is browned, asparagus just tender and fish is cooked as desired. Serve fish with potato, asparagus and sauce.
tarragon sauce Melt butter in small saucepan; cook onion, stirring, until soft. Add wine; bring to the boil then simmer, uncovered, until liquid reduces by half. Add cream; simmer, uncovered, about 10 minutes or until sauce thickens slightly. Remove from heat; stir in tarragon.

HONEYED GINGER FISH BUNDLES

prep & cook time **30 minutes** serves **4**
nutritional count per serving **2.5g total fat (0.7g saturated fat); 531kJ (127 cal); 4.5g carbohydrate; 21g protein; 0.8g fibre**

4 x 100g firm white fish fillets
1 tablespoon japanese soy sauce
2 teaspoons honey
¼ teaspoon sesame oil
1 small carrot (70g), cut into matchsticks
3 green onions, sliced thinly
3cm piece fresh ginger (15g), cut into matchsticks
4 fresh coriander sprigs

honeyed ginger fish bundles

1 Preheat oven to 200°C/180°C fan-forced.
2 Place each fillet on 20cm squares of baking paper or foil. Combine sauce, honey and oil in small jug; pour mixture over fish. Top with combined carrot, onion and ginger. Gather corners of baking paper together above fish; twist to enclose securely.
3 Place parcels on oven tray; bake 15 minutes. Stand fish 5 minutes before serving topped with coriander.
serve with **steamed jasmine rice.**
note **We used coral trout in this recipe, but you can use any firm fish fillets you like.**

BREAM IN MACADAMIA BUTTER

prep & cook time **15 minutes** serves **4**
nutritional count per serving **40.4g total fat (16.3g saturated fat); 2211kJ (529 cal); 1g carbohydrate; 40.8g protein; 1.3g fibre**

Dry-fry ½ cup macadamias in large frying pan over low heat, shaking pan constantly, until fragrant; remove from heat. When cool enough to handle, chop nuts coarsely. Melt 80g butter in same pan; cook nuts and ⅓ cup finely chopped fresh coriander, stirring, 1 minute. Add four 200g bream fillets to pan; cook, turning halfway through cooking, until cooked through. Serve fish drizzled with butter.
serve with **steamed baby green beans.**

CAJUN FISH

prep & cook time **15 minutes** serves **4**
nutritional count per serving **7.4g total fat (2g saturated fat); 1313kJ (314 cal); 12.2g carbohydrate; 46.6g protein; 5.3g fibre**

Combine 2 teaspoons each sweet paprika, ground cumin, ground coriander, mustard powder and fennel seeds with ¼ teaspoon cayenne pepper in small bowl. Rub mixture into four 200g kingfish fillets; cook fish in heated oiled large frying pan until cooked as desired, remove from pan. Heat 2 teaspoons olive oil in same cleaned pan; cook 1 sliced small red onion and 1 chopped large tomato until soft. Add 420g can rinsed, drained kidney beans; stir until hot. Divide bean mixture among plates; top with fish.
serve with **coleslaw.**
note **We used kingfish in this recipe, but you can use any firm white fish you like.**

15-MINUTE MEALS

SMOKED TROUT, BRIE AND CRANBERRY SALAD

prep time **10 minutes** serves **4**
nutritional count per serving **19.8g total fat (7g saturated fat); 1095kJ (262 cal); 1.4g carbohydrate; 19.3g protein; 0.7g fibre**

Divide 350g trimmed watercress, 200g flaked smoked trout and 110g sliced brie cheese among four plates. Combine 2 tablespoons each of olive oil and cranberry juice and 1 tablespoon lemon juice in screw-top jar; shake well. Drizzle dressing over salad.

TUNA AND CHILLI PASTA

prep & cook time **15 minutes** serves **4**
nutritional count per serving **22.3g total fat (3.2g saturated fat); 2617kJ (626 cal); 67.5g carbohydrate; 32.5g protein; 4.8g fibre**

Cook 375g angel hair pasta in large saucepan of boiling water until tender; drain, reserving ¼ cup cooking liquid. Rinse pasta under cold water, drain. Meanwhile, drain 425g can tuna in oil, reserving 2 tablespoons of the oil. Heat oil in medium frying pan, add four thinly sliced garlic cloves; cook, stirring, until fragrant. Add 1 teaspoon dried chilli flakes and ⅓ cup white wine; cook, uncovered, until wine is almost evaporated. Add undrained 400g can chopped tomatoes, tuna and reserved cooking liquid; simmer until liquid has reduced slightly. Remove from heat; stir in 1 tablespoon lemon juice. Combine pasta and sauce in large bowl.

WARM SALMON, RISONI AND PEA SALAD

prep & cook time **30 minutes** serves **4**
nutritional count per serving **23.6g total fat (4.1g saturated fat); 2324kJ (556 cal); 49g carbohydrate; 3.6g protein; 7.8g fibre**

250g risoni pasta
2 cups (240g) frozen peas
1 tablespoon olive oil
500g salmon fillets
8 green onions, sliced thickly
100g baby spinach leaves
dill dressing
2 tablespoons olive oil
2 teaspoons finely grated lemon rind
¼ cup (60ml) lemon juice
1 teaspoon dijon mustard
1 tablespoon coarsely chopped fresh dill

1 Cook pasta in large saucepan of boiling water until almost tender. Add peas to pan with pasta towards the end of pasta cooking time and cook until peas and pasta are just tender; drain.
2 Meanwhile, make dill dressing.
3 Heat oil in large frying pan; cook fish, uncovered, until cooked as desired. Remove from pan; stand 5 minutes. Discard skin and any bones. Flake fish into large chunks.
4 Place pasta, peas and fish in large bowl with onion, spinach and dressing; toss gently.
dill dressing Combine ingredients in screw-top jar; shake well.

asian smoked trout salad with sambal dressing

ASIAN SMOKED TROUT SALAD WITH SAMBAL DRESSING

prep & cook time **20 minutes** serves **4**
nutritional count per serving **6.6g total fat (1.2g saturated fat); 1062kJ (254 cal); 25.9g carbohydrate; 21.6g protein; 1.5g fibre**

125g rice vermicelli
2 x 150g smoked ocean trout portions, skinned, flaked
1 small carrot (70g), cut into matchstick-sized pieces
1 lebanese cucumber (130g), cut into matchstick-sized pieces

sambal dressing

1 tablespoon sambal oelek
1 tablespoon brown sugar
1 tablespoon fish sauce
¼ cup (60ml) lime juice
2 teaspoons sesame oil

1 Place vermicelli in large heatproof bowl, cover with boiling water; stand until tender, drain. Rinse under cold water; drain. Using scissors, cut vermicelli into random lengths.
2 Meanwhile, make sambal dressing.
3 Combine vermicelli, fish, carrot, cucumber and dressing in large bowl.
sambal dressing Combine ingredients in small bowl.

SALT & SICHUAN PEPPER SALMON WITH WASABI MAYONNAISE

prep & cook time **25 minutes** serves **4**
nutritional count per serving **40.1g total fat (6.3g saturated fat); 2278kJ (545 cal); 7.5g carbohydrate; 39.4 protein; 0.2g fibre**

2 teaspoons sea salt
2 teaspoons sichuan pepper
¼ cup (60ml) vegetable oil
4 x 200g salmon fillets, skin on
½ cup (150g) mayonnaise
2 teaspoons wasabi paste
1 teaspoon finely chopped fresh coriander
1 teaspoon lime juice

salt & sichuan pepper salmon with wasabi mayonnaise

1 Using mortar and pestle or pepper grinder, grind salt and pepper until fine. Combine pepper mixture, half the oil and fish in large bowl, cover; stand 5 minutes.
2 Meanwhile, combine mayonnaise, wasabi, coriander and juice in small bowl.
3 Heat remaining oil in large frying pan; cook fish, skin-side down, until skin crisps. Turn fish; cook, uncovered, until cooked as desired. Serve fish with wasabi mayonnaise.
serve with **watercress.**

LEMONY MUSSELS WITH GINGER

prep & cook time **35 minutes** serves **4**
nutritional count per serving **2.7g total fat (0.4g saturated fat); 719kJ (172 cal); 20.1g carbohydrate; 10.2g protein; 4g fibre**

- ⅔ cup (130g) jasmine rice
- 1⅓ cups (330ml) water
- 1kg small black mussels
- 1 teaspoon sesame oil
- 4cm piece fresh ginger (20g), grated
- 10cm stick fresh lemon grass (20g), chopped finely
- 2 fresh small red thai chillies, sliced thinly
- 2 cloves garlic, crushed
- ⅓ cup (80ml) chinese cooking wine
- 2 tablespoons mirin
- 1 tablespoon kecap manis
- 4 green onions, sliced thinly
- 6 baby buk choy (900g), halved lengthways

1 Rinse rice under cold water until water runs clear; drain.
2 Bring the water to the boil, covered, in medium saucepan; add rice. Cook, covered, over low heat, 10 minutes. Remove from heat; stand, covered, 10 minutes. Fluff rice with fork.
3 Meanwhile, scrub mussels under cold water; remove beards.
4 Heat oil in large saucepan; cook ginger, lemon grass, chilli and garlic, stirring, until fragrant. Add mussels and cooking wine; cook, covered tightly, about 5 minutes or until mussels open (discard any that do not).
5 Stir mirin, kecap manis and onion into mussel mixture. Divide buk choy among serving bowls; top with hot mussel mixture. Serve mussels with rice.

prawn and grilled capsicum pizzas

PRAWN AND GRILLED CAPSICUM PIZZAS

prep & cook time **30 minutes** serves **4**
nutritional count per serving **16.9g total fat (4.4g saturated fat); 2328kJ (557 cal); 62.6g carbohydrate; 35.1g protein; 5.7g fibre**

720g uncooked medium king prawns
1 tablespoon olive oil
4 cloves garlic, crushed
2 fresh small red thai chillies, chopped finely
4 x 112g pizza bases
⅓ cup (95g) tomato paste
½ cup (50g) coarsely grated mozzarella cheese
270g jar char-grilled capsicum in oil, drained, chopped coarsely
¼ cup (20g) flaked parmesan cheese
⅓ cup loosely packed fresh basil leaves

1 Preheat oven to 220°C/200°C fan-forced. Oil two oven trays.
2 Shell and devein prawns; combine with oil, garlic and chilli in large bowl.
3 Cook prawn mixture in heated large frying pan until prawns are changed in colour.
4 Spread pizza bases with paste; top with mozzarella, prawns and capsicum. Cook, uncovered, about 15 minutes. Sprinkle pizzas with parmesan and basil.

note **We used small (15cm diameter) packaged pizza bases for this recipe.**

TUNA SALAD

prep time **15 minutes** serves **4**
nutritional count per serving **26.1g total fat (4.9g saturated fat); 1492kJ (357 cal); 4.6g carbohydrate; 24.4g protein; 4.9g fibre**

¼ cup (60ml) olive oil
2 tablespoons white wine vinegar
1 tablespoon lemon juice
2 teaspoons finely chopped fresh basil
2 teaspoons finely chopped fresh oregano
1 clove garlic, crushed
1 fresh long red chilli, chopped finely
1 medium iceberg lettuce, cut into wedges
425g can tuna in springwater, drained, flaked
250g cherry tomatoes, halved

tuna salad

1 medium avocado (250g), chopped coarsely
1 lebanese cucumber (130g), sliced thinly
1 small red onion (100g), sliced thinly

1 Combine oil, vinegar, juice, herbs, garlic and chilli in screw-top jar; shake well.
2 Place lettuce wedges on serving plate; top with remaining ingredients. Drizzle with dressing.

TAMARIND AND LIME SNAPPER

prep & cook time **25 minutes** serves **4**
nutritional count per serving **2.6g total fat (0.9g saturated fat); 1145kJ (275 cal); 28g carbohydrate; 33.3g protein; 0.9g fibre**

⅔ cup (130g) jasmine rice
1⅓ cups (330ml) water
4 x 150g snapper fillets
1 lime, sliced thinly
2 green onions, sliced thinly
tamarind lime dressing
2 tablespoons water
2 tablespoons tamarind concentrate
1 tablespoon fish sauce
1 tablespoon lime juice
2 teaspoons brown sugar
1 fresh small red thai chilli, chopped finely

1 Rinse rice under cold water until water runs clear; drain.
2 Bring the water to the boil, covered, in medium saucepan; add rice. Cook, covered, over low heat, 10 minutes. Remove from heat; stand, covered, 10 minutes. Fluff rice with fork.
3 Meanwhile, place fish, in single layer, in large baking-paper-lined bamboo steamer; top with lime slices. Place steamer over large saucepan of simmering water; steam fish about 8 minutes or until cooked through.
4 Meanwhile, make tamarind lime dressing.
5 Divide rice among serving plates; top with fish, onion and dressing.
tamarind lime dressing Combine ingredients in small saucepan; bring to the boil. Boil, uncovered, about 2 minutes or until dressing has thickened slightly.

barbecued octopus with tomato salad

BARBECUED OCTOPUS WITH TOMATO SALAD

prep & cook time **25 minutes** serves **4**
nutritional count per serving **1.9g total fat (0g saturated fat); 681kJ (163 cal); 6.9g carbohydrate; 27.4g protein; 3.4g fibre**

600g baby octopus
1 teaspoon finely grated lemon rind
2 tablespoons lemon juice
2 teaspoons finely chopped fresh oregano
1 clove garlic, crushed
½ teaspoon cracked black pepper
cooking-oil spray
tomato salad
4 medium tomatoes (600g), seeded, chopped coarsely
2 lebanese cucumbers (260g), chopped coarsely
1 small red onion (100g), chopped finely
1 small green capsicum (150g), chopped coarsely
1 tablespoon coarsely chopped fresh oregano leaves
1 tablespoon white wine vinegar

1 Make tomato salad.
2 Combine octopus, rind, juice, oregano, garlic and pepper in medium bowl.
3 Lightly spray heated barbecue grill plate with oil. Cook octopus, turning occasionally, until cooked through.
4 Serve octopus with tomato salad, and lemon wedges, if you like.
tomato salad Combine ingredients in medium bowl; toss gently.

pan-fried fish with fennel salad

PAN-FRIED FISH WITH FENNEL SALAD

prep & cook time **20 minutes** serves **4**
nutritional count per serving **13.9g total fat (2.7g saturated fat); 1409kJ (337 cal); 8.6g carbohydrate; 42.9g protein; 2.8g fibre**

4 x 200g firm white fish fillets, skin-on
2 medium red capsicums (400g), chopped coarsely
2 small fennel bulbs (400g), trimmed, sliced thinly
½ cup (60g) seeded black olives
⅓ cup coarsely chopped fresh basil
2 tablespoons olive oil
1 tablespoon balsamic vinegar

1 Cook fish, skin-side down, in heated oiled large frying pan, turning once, until cooked.
2 Meanwhile, combine remaining ingredients in medium bowl. Serve fish with salad.
note **We used blue-eye fillets, but any firm white fish fillet will do.**

TURKISH CHICKEN CLUB

prep & cook time 30 minutes **makes** 4
nutritional count per sandwich 32.1g total fat (5.4g saturated fat); 2700kJ (646 cal); 57.5g carbohydrate; 29.6g protein; 4.6g fibre

⅓ cup (80ml) lime juice
2 tablespoons olive oil
2 teaspoons sumac
2 chicken thigh fillets (400g)
1 large turkish bread (430g)
1 lebanese cucumber (130g), sliced thinly
1 medium tomato (150g), sliced thinly
24 small butter lettuce leaves

coriander aïoli
½ cup (150g) mayonnaise
1 tablespoon lime juice
1 clove garlic, crushed
2 tablespoons finely chopped fresh coriander

1 Combine juice, oil, sumac and chicken in medium bowl.
2 Make coriander aïoli.
3 Drain chicken; reserve marinade. Cook chicken on heated oiled grill plate (or grill or barbecue) until cooked through, brushing with reserved marinade after turning. Cover; stand 5 minutes then slice thinly.
4 Halve bread horizontally; cut each piece into 6 slices. Toast slices lightly.
5 Spread each toast slice with aïoli. Layer 4 toast slices with half the chicken, cucumber, tomato and lettuce, then top with toasts; layer with remaining chicken, cucumber, tomato and lettuce then top with remaining toast. Cut in half to serve, if you like.
coriander aïoli Place ingredients in small bowl; mix until combined.
note You will need two butter lettuces for this recipe.

POULTRY

smoked chicken salad with wild rice

SMOKED CHICKEN SALAD WITH WILD RICE

prep & cook time **25 minutes** serves **6**
nutritional count per serving **33.9g total fat (5.1g saturated fat); 2851kJ (682 cal); 61.9g carbohydrate; 29.1g protein; 6.4g fibre**

2 cups (400g) wild rice blend
200g seedless red grapes
3 stalks celery (450g), trimmed, sliced thinly
½ cup (60g) roasted pecans
350g watercress, trimmed
500g smoked chicken breasts, sliced thinly
lime and black pepper dressing
½ cup (125ml) lime juice
½ cup (125ml) olive oil
1 tablespoon caster sugar
¼ teaspoon cracked black pepper

1 Cook rice in large saucepan of boiling water, uncovered, until just tender; drain. Rinse under cold water; drain.
2 Make lime and black pepper dressing.
3 Place rice in large bowl with grapes, celery, nuts and half the dressing; toss gently.
4 Divide watercress among serving plates; top with rice salad then chicken. Drizzle with remaining dressing.
lime and black pepper dressing Combine ingredients in screw-top jar; shake well.

STUFFED CHICKEN BREAST WITH SPINACH SALAD

prep & cook time **30 minutes** serves **4**
nutritional count per serving **15.9g total fat (5.8g saturated fat); 1584kJ (379 cal); 10.6g carbohydrate; 46.2g protein; 3.8g fibre**

4 chicken breast fillets (800g)
80g fontina cheese, sliced thinly
4 slices bottled char-grilled red capsicum (170g)
100g baby spinach leaves
1 medium lemon (140g)
2 medium oranges (480g)
1 small red onion (100g), sliced thinly
1 tablespoon olive oil

stuffed chicken breast with spinach salad

1 Using tip of a small knife, slit a pocket in one side of each fillet, taking care not to cut all the way through. Divide cheese, capsicum and a few spinach leaves among pockets; secure with toothpicks.
2 Cook chicken on heated oiled grill plate (or grill or barbecue), uncovered, until cooked through. Cover chicken; stand 10 minutes. Remove toothpicks; slice thickly.
3 Meanwhile, segment lemon and orange over large bowl; add onion, oil and remaining spinach; toss gently.
4 Serve chicken with salad.

HERBED CHICKEN SCHNITZEL

prep & cook time **35 minutes** serves **4**
nutritional count per serving **28.1g total fat (5.9g saturated fat); 2746kJ (657 cal); 38.5g carbohydrate; 59.9g protein; 4.6g fibre**

4 chicken breast fillets (800g)
¼ cup (35g) plain flour
2 eggs
1 tablespoon milk
2½ cups (175g) stale white breadcrumbs
2 teaspoons finely grated lemon rind
2 tablespoons finely chopped fresh flat-leaf parsley
2 tablespoons finely chopped fresh basil
⅓ cup (25g) finely grated parmesan cheese
vegetable oil, for shallow-frying

green bean salad
250g baby green beans, trimmed
2 tablespoons lemon juice
1 tablespoon olive oil
⅓ cup coarsely chopped fresh flat-leaf parsley

1 Using meat mallet, gently pound chicken, one piece at a time, between sheets of plastic wrap until 5mm thick; cut each piece in half.
2 Whisk flour, eggs and milk in shallow bowl; combine breadcrumbs, rind, herbs and cheese in another shallow bowl. Coat chicken pieces, one at a time, in egg then breadcrumb mixture.
3 Heat oil in large frying pan; shallow-fry chicken, in batches, until cooked. Drain on absorbent paper.
4 Meanwhile, make green bean salad; serve salad with chicken.

green bean salad Boil, steam or microwave beans until tender; drain. Toss beans in medium bowl with remaining ingredients.

chicken singapore noodles

CHICKEN SINGAPORE NOODLES

prep & cook time **25 minutes** serves **4**
nutritional count per serving **19.1g total fat (6.4g saturated fat); 2057kJ (492 cal); 27.3g carbohydrate; 49.1g protein; 5.8g fibre**

450g fresh singapore noodles
2 teaspoons sesame oil
2 cloves garlic, crushed
2cm piece fresh ginger (10g), grated
1 medium carrot (120g), cut into matchsticks
250g cooked shelled small prawns
1 tablespoon malaysian curry powder
3 green onions, sliced thinly
1½ cups bean sprouts (120g)
2 tablespoons soy sauce
¼ cup (60ml) kecap manis
3 cups (480g) shredded barbecued chicken

1 Place noodles in large heatproof bowl, cover with boiling water; separate with fork, drain.
2 Meanwhile, heat oil in wok; stir-fry garlic, ginger and carrot until carrot is just tender. Add prawns and curry powder; stir-fry until prawns change colour.
3 Add noodles and remaining ingredients; stir-fry until hot.

pesto chicken with grilled zucchini

PESTO CHICKEN WITH GRILLED ZUCCHINI

prep & cook time **25 minutes** serves **4**
nutritional count per serving **33.1g total fat (7.6g saturated fat); 2611kJ (481 cal); 3.3g carbohydrate; 41.7g protein; 3.6g fibre**

6 medium zucchini (720g), sliced thickly lengthways
2 tablespoons olive oil
1 clove garlic, crushed
1 tablespoon finely chopped fresh basil
1 teaspoon finely grated lemon rind
⅓ cup (90g) sun-dried tomato pesto
2 tablespoons chicken stock
4 x 200g chicken thigh fillets, cut into thirds

1 Cook zucchini on heated oiled grill plate (or grill or barbecue), in batches, until tender. Combine with oil, garlic, basil and rind in medium bowl; cover to keep warm.
2 Combine pesto, stock and chicken in large bowl. Cook chicken on heated oiled grill plate, brushing occasionally with pesto mixture, until cooked through. Serve chicken with zucchini.

FARFALLE WITH CHICKEN, RICOTTA, SPINACH AND TOMATOES

prep & cook time **25 minutes** serves **4**
nutritional count per serving **20.7g total fat (7.7g saturated fat); 2851kJ (682 cal); 67.7g carbohydrate; 52.2g protein; 5.6g fibre**

375g farfalle pasta
1 tablespoon olive oil
1 medium brown onion (150g), chopped finely
1 clove garlic, crushed
600g chicken tenderloins, chopped coarsely
150g baby spinach leaves
1 cup (240g) ricotta cheese
1 egg
2 teaspoons finely grated lemon rind
2 tablespoons lemon juice
200g grape tomatoes, halved
¼ cup (20g) finely grated parmesan cheese

1 Cook pasta in large saucepan of boiling water until just tender; drain.
2 Meanwhile, heat oil in large deep frying pan; cook onion and garlic, stirring, until onion softens. Add chicken; cook, stirring, over medium heat, about 5 minutes or until cooked through.
3 Place chicken mixture, spinach, combined ricotta and egg, rind, juice, tomato and drained pasta in large serving bowl; toss gently. Sprinkle with grated parmesan to serve.

note **Farfalle is a bow-tie shaped short pasta; it is sometimes known as butterfly pasta.**

spinach and ricotta-stuffed chicken parmigiana

SPINACH AND RICOTTA-STUFFED CHICKEN PARMIGIANA

prep & cook time **35 minutes** serves **4**
nutritional count per serving **40.2g total fat (15.3g saturated fat); 3194kJ (764 cal); 31.9g carbohydrate; 67.2g protein; 2.9g fibre**

8 x 100g chicken schnitzels (*see note, below*)
40g baby spinach leaves
1⅓ cups (320g) ricotta cheese
¼ cup (35g) plain flour
2 eggs
2 tablespoons milk
1½ cups (105g) stale breadcrumbs
vegetable oil, for shallow-frying
1 cup (260g) bottled tomato pasta sauce
1 cup (100g) coarsely grated mozzarella cheese

1 Preheat oven to 200°C/180°C fan-forced.
2 Top each schnitzel with spinach and cheese, leaving 1cm border around edges. Fold in half to secure filling; press down firmly.
3 Coat schnitzels in flour; shake off excess. Dip, one at a time, in combined egg and milk, then in breadcrumbs.
4 Heat oil in large frying pan; cook schnitzels, in batches, until browned and cooked through. Drain on absorbent paper.
5 Place schnitzels in oiled shallow large baking dish; top with sauce and cheese. Roast, in oven, uncovered, about 10 minutes or until cheese melts.

note **We use plain chicken schnitzels, not crumbed. Plain schnitzels are available from poultry shops and some supermarkets. You can make your own by cutting breast fillets horizontally into thin slices, then pounding them between layers of plastic wrap until they are thin and of an even thickness.**

ginger plum chicken and noodle stir-fry

GINGER PLUM CHICKEN AND NOODLE STIR-FRY

prep & cook time **25 minutes** serves **4**
nutritional count per serving **19.4g total fat (4.6g saturated fat); 2784kJ (666 cal); 73.3g carbohydrate; 45.6g protein; 6.2g fibre**

2 tablespoons vegetable oil
600g chicken breast fillets, sliced thinly
450g hokkien noodles
1 medium brown onion (150g), sliced thinly
1 clove garlic, crushed
3cm piece fresh ginger (15g), grated
400g packaged fresh asian stir-fry vegetables
2 tablespoons sweet chilli sauce
2 tablespoons plum sauce

1 Heat half the oil in wok; stir-fry chicken, in batches, until browned. Remove from wok.
2 Meanwhile, place noodles in medium heatproof bowl, cover with boiling water; separate with fork, drain.
3 Heat remaining oil in wok; stir-fry onion, garlic and ginger until onion softens. Add vegetables; stir-fry until just tender. Return chicken to wok with noodles and sauces; stir-fry until hot.

chicken, tomato and fetta patties with spinach salad

CHICKEN, TOMATO AND FETTA PATTIES WITH SPINACH SALAD

prep & cook time **30 minutes** serves **4**
nutritional count per serving **33.7g total fat (13.3g saturated fat); 2320kJ (555 cal); 11.8g carbohydrate; 50.1g protein; 3.2g fibre**

750g chicken mince
⅓ cup (50g) drained semi-dried tomatoes, chopped coarsely
1 egg
½ cup (35g) stale breadcrumbs
200g fetta cheese, crumbled
1 small white onion (80g), sliced thinly
100g baby spinach leaves
1 tablespoon olive oil
1 tablespoon balsamic vinegar

1 Combine chicken, tomato, egg, breadcrumbs and half the cheese in large bowl; shape mixture into 12 patties.
2 Cook patties in heated oiled large frying pan, in batches, until cooked through. Drain on absorbent paper.
3 Meanwhile, combine onion, spinach, oil, vinegar and remaining cheese in medium bowl. Serve patties with spinach salad.

SATAY CHICKEN PIZZAS WITH ROCKET AND RAITA

prep & cook time **35 minutes** serves **4**
nutritional count per serving **48.1g total fat (16.3g saturated fat); 4301kJ (1029 cal); 73.1g carbohydrate; 70.5g protein; 10.6g fibre**

½ cup (140g) crunchy peanut butter
½ cup (125ml) sweet chilli sauce
4 x 15cm prepared pizza bases
3 cups (480g) shredded barbecued chicken
200g provolone cheese, grated coarsely
50g baby rocket leaves
raita
1 lebanese cucumber (130g), chopped finely
1 small brown onion (80g), chopped finely
½ cup (140g) yogurt
2 tablespoons finely chopped fresh mint
1 long green chilli, chopped finely

1 Preheat oven to 200°C/180°C fan-forced.
2 Combine peanut butter and chilli sauce in small bowl.
3 Place pizza bases on oven trays; spread sauce mixture evenly over each base. Divide chicken and cheese among bases; bake about 15 minutes or until pizza tops brown and bases crisp.
4 Meanwhile, make raita.
5 Serve pizza topped with raita and rocket.
raita Combine ingredients in small bowl.

satay chicken pizzas with rocket and raita

MOROCCAN CHICKEN PIZZETTA

prep & cook time **15 minutes** serves **4**
nutritional count per serving **22.7g total fat (7g saturated fat); 2679kJ (641 cal); 64.3g carbohydrate; 40.2g protein; 8.6g fibre**

Preheat oven to 220°C/200°C fan-forced. Place four small pizza bases on oven trays. Spread bases with ⅔ cup hummus; top with 2 cups shredded barbecued chicken, 120g rinsed and thinly sliced preserved lemon then 120g thinly sliced haloumi cheese. Bake about 8 minutes. Serve pizzettas sprinkled with ⅓ cup loosely packed fresh flat-leaf parsley leaves and 1 tablespoon olive oil.

note **You need to buy a medium barbecued chicken for this recipe.**

GRILLED CHICKEN, BRIE AND AVOCADO ON CIABATTA

prep & cook time **15 minutes** serves **4**
nutritional count per serving **22.6g total fat (8.3g saturated fat); 1768kJ (423 cal); 22.9g carbohydrate; 30.6g protein; 2.9g fibre**

Halve two 200g chicken breast fillets diagonally; slice through each piece horizontally (you will have 8 pieces). Cook chicken on heated oiled grill plate (or grill or barbecue) until cooked. Toast four thick slices ciabatta bread, both sides, on grill plate. Spread 2 tablespoons sweet chilli sauce over toast slices; top with 50g baby rocket leaves, chicken, 100g sliced brie cheese then 1 thinly sliced small avocado. Drizzle with another 2 tablespoons sweet chilli sauce.

15-MINUTE MEALS

CHICKEN MASALA WITH COCONUT RAITA

prep & cook time **15 minutes** serves **4**
nutritional count per serving **20.4g total fat (6.7g saturated fat); 1714kJ (410 cal); 6g carbohydrate; 49.1g protein; 2.3g fibre**

Combine four 200g chicken breast fillets with 1 tablespoon vegetable oil and ¼ cup tikka masala paste in medium bowl. Cook chicken in heated oiled large frying pan until cooked through. Meanwhile, make raita by combining ⅓ cup flaked coconut, ¾ cup greek-style yogurt, 1 teaspoon finely grated lime rind and 1 tablespoon lime juice in small bowl. Top chicken with raita.

serve with **steamed basmati rice and pappadums.**

CHICKEN WITH PROSCIUTTO AND CAPERS

prep & cook time **15 minutes** serves **4**
nutritional count per serving **17.8g total fat (9.6g saturated fat); 1492kJ (357 cal); 0.9g carbohydrate; 48.1g protein; 0.3g fibre**

Wrap one slice of prosciutto tightly around each of four 200g chicken breast fillets. Cook chicken in heated oiled large frying pan until cooked through; remove from pan, cover to keep warm. Melt 60g butter in same pan; add 2 tablespoons rinsed drained baby capers, 1 crushed garlic clove, 1 tablespoon finely chopped fresh basil and 1 tablespoon finely chopped fresh flat-leaf parsley. Cook, stirring gently, until herbs just wilt. Top chicken with warm herb sauce.

STEAK DIANE

prep & cook time 20 minutes **serves** 4
nutritional count per serving 39.1g total fat (21.6g saturated fat); 2182kJ (522 cal); 5.2g carbohydrate; 27.9g protein; 0.4g fibre

1 tablespoon olive oil
4 x 125g beef fillet steaks
⅓ cup (80ml) brandy
2 cloves garlic, crushed
¼ cup (60ml) worcestershire sauce
1 cup (250ml) cream
1 tablespoon finely chopped fresh flat-leaf parsley

1 Heat oil in large frying pan; cook steaks. Remove from pan; cover to keep warm.
2 Add brandy to pan; bring to the boil. Add garlic, sauce and cream; cook, stirring, about 3 minutes or until sauce thickens slightly.
3 Remove from heat; stir in parsley. Top steaks with sauce to serve.

serve with shoestring chips and a leafy green salad.

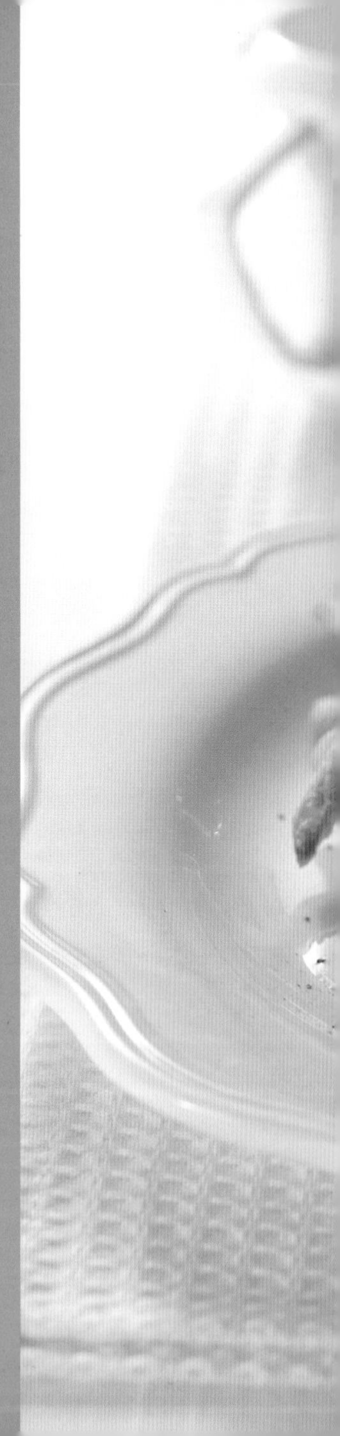

MEAT

peppered fillet steaks with creamy bourbon sauce

PEPPERED FILLET STEAKS WITH CREAMY BOURBON SAUCE

prep & cook time **20 minutes** serves **4**
nutritional count per serving **49.3g total fat (25.9g saturated fat); 2742kJ (656 cal); 13.2g carbohydrate; 28.7g protein; 0.7g fibre**

4 x 125g beef fillet steaks
2 teaspoons cracked black pepper
2 tablespoons olive oil
6 shallots (150g), sliced thinly
1 clove garlic, crushed
⅓ cup (80ml) bourbon
¼ cup (60ml) beef stock
2 teaspoons dijon mustard
300ml cream

1 Rub beef all over with pepper. Heat half the oil in large frying pan; cook beef, uncovered, until cooked as desired. Remove from pan; cover to keep warm.
2 Heat remaining oil in same pan; cook shallot and garlic, stirring, until shallot softens. Add bourbon; stir until mixture simmers and starts to thicken. Add remaining ingredients; bring to the boil. Reduce heat; simmer, uncovered, about 5 minutes or until sauce thickens slightly.
3 Serve beef drizzled with sauce.
serve with **steamed green beans and home-made potato chips.**

chilli jam beef stir-fry

CHILLI JAM BEEF STIR-FRY

prep & cook time **20 minutes** serves **4**
nutritional count per serving **24.7g total fat (7g saturated fat); 2057kJ (492 cal); 19.6g carbohydrate; 46.4g protein; 3g fibre**

2 tablespoons vegetable oil
800g beef strips
1 medium brown onion (150g), chopped coarsely
2 cloves garlic, crushed
115g baby corn, halved lengthways
150g snow peas, halved crossways
½ cup (160g) chilli jam
2 teaspoons finely grated lime rind
2 tablespoons lime juice

1 Heat half the oil in wok; cook beef, in batches, until browned. Remove from wok.
2 Heat remaining oil in wok; cook onion and garlic, stirring, until onion softens. Add corn; cook, stirring, until corn is just tender.
3 Return beef to wok with peas, jam, rind and juice; stir-fry until sauce thickens slightly.

STEAK SANDWICH

prep & cook time **30 minutes** makes **4**
nutritional count per sandwich **20.5g total fat (5g saturated fat); 2809kJ (672 cal); 78.1g carbohydrate; 39.7g protein; 6.4g fibre**

2 cloves garlic, crushed
2 tablespoons olive oil
4 thin beef scotch fillet steaks (500g)
2 medium brown onions (300g), sliced thinly
1 tablespoon brown sugar
1 tablespoon balsamic vinegar
8 thick slices white bread (560g)
1 baby cos lettuce (180g), leaves separated
2 dill pickles (40g) sliced thinly
¼ cup (80g) tomato chutney

1 Combine garlic and half the oil in medium bowl; add steaks, rub both sides with mixture.
2 Heat remaining oil in medium frying pan; cook onion over low heat, stirring occasionally, about 10 minutes or until soft. Add sugar and vinegar; cook, stirring, about 5 minutes or until caramelised. Remove from pan.
3 Meanwhile, cook steaks in heated oiled large frying pan.
4 Toast bread both sides. Sandwich lettuce, steaks, onion, pickle and chutney between toast slices.

note **We used white sourdough bread in this recipe.**

veal saltimbocca

VEAL SALTIMBOCCA

prep & cook time **35 minutes** serves **4**
nutritional count per serving **24g total fat (13.1g saturated fat); 2312kJ (553 cal); 9g carbohydrate; 63.3g protein; 3.6g fibre**

8 veal schnitzels (800g)
8 slices prosciutto (120g)
4 bocconcini cheese (240g), sliced thinly
⅔ cup (100g) drained semi-dried tomatoes
16 fresh sage leaves
40g butter
1 cup (250ml) dry white wine
1 tablespoon lemon juice
2 tablespoons coarsely chopped fresh sage

1 Top each piece of veal with prosciutto, cheese, tomatoes and sage leaves. Fold in half and secure with toothpicks or small skewers.
2 Melt half the butter in medium frying pan; cook veal, in batches, until cooked as desired. Remove from pan; cover to keep warm.
3 Add wine to pan; bring to the boil. Boil, uncovered, until wine reduces by half. Stir in remaining butter, juice and sage.
4 Serve saltimbocca drizzled with sauce.
note **Veal schnitzel is thinly sliced steak available crumbed or plain (uncrumbed); we use plain schnitzel, sometimes called escalopes, in our recipes.**

chilli lamb stir-fry

CHILLI LAMB STIR-FRY

prep & cook time **35 minutes** serves **4**
nutritional count per serving **13.9g total fat (3.7g saturated fat); 1154kJ (276 cal); 8.7g carbohydrate; 28.4g protein; 1.6g fibre**

2 tablespoons peanut oil
500g lamb fillets, sliced thinly
4cm piece fresh ginger (20g), sliced thinly
1 large brown onion (200g), sliced thickly
1 large red capsicum (350g), sliced thickly
2 tablespoons water
1 teaspoon dried chilli flakes
2 tablespoons oyster sauce
2 tablespoons light soy sauce

1 Heat half the oil in wok; stir-fry lamb, in batches, until browned. Remove from wok.
2 Heat remaining oil in wok; stir-fry ginger, onion and capsicum, 5 minutes. Add the water; cook, covered, about 10 minutes or until vegetables soften.
3 Return lamb to wok with chilli and sauces; stir-fry, 2 minutes or until heated through.

ZA'ATAR-CRUSTED KEBABS WITH HUMMUS

prep & cook time **30 minutes** serves **4**
nutritional count per serving **50g total fat (13.1g saturated fat); 4673kJ (1118 cal); 89.7g carbohydrate; 70.2g protein; 13.9g fibre**

1 tablespoon olive oil
1 tablespoon lemon juice
800g diced lamb
8 pieces lavash
½ cup coarsely chopped fresh flat-leaf parsley
200g yogurt

hummus

2 x 300g cans chickpeas, rinsed, drained
1 clove garlic, quartered
½ cup (140g) tahini
½ cup (125ml) lemon juice
½ cup (125ml) water

za'atar

1 tablespoon sumac
1 tablespoon toasted sesame seeds
1 teaspoon dried marjoram
2 teaspoons dried thyme

1 Combine oil and juice in medium bowl, add lamb; toss lamb to coat in mixture. Thread lamb onto skewers.
2 Make hummus.
3 Make za'atar. Spread za'atar on tray. Roll kebabs in za'atar until coated all over. Cook kebabs on heated oiled grill plate (or grill or barbecue), uncovered, until cooked as desired. Serve kebabs on lavash with hummus, parsley and yogurt.

hummus Blend or process ingredients until smooth. Cover; refrigerate until required.

za'atar Combine ingredients in small bowl.

note **You need eight bamboo skewers for this recipe; soak them in cold water for 30 minutes before using to prevent them from scorching during cooking.**

veal with salsa verde and potato rösti

VEAL WITH SALSA VERDE AND POTATO RÖSTI

prep & cook time **35 minutes** serves **4**
nutritional count per serving **33.1g total fat (5.2g saturated fat); 2500kJ (598 cal); 22.7g carbohydrate; 50.7g protein; 3.6g fibre**

800g piece veal tenderloin, halved lengthways
4 medium potatoes (800g)
1 egg

salsa verde

⅔ cup finely chopped fresh flat-leaf parsley
⅓ cup finely chopped fresh mint
⅓ cup finely chopped fresh dill
⅓ cup finely chopped fresh chives
1 tablespoon wholegrain mustard
¼ cup (60ml) lemon juice
¼ cup (50g) drained baby capers, rinsed
2 cloves garlic, crushed
½ cup (125ml) olive oil

1 Make salsa verde.
2 Rub veal with half the salsa; cook on heated oiled flat plate, uncovered, until cooked as you like. Remove from heat; cover to keep warm.
3 To make rösti, grate potatoes coarsely then squeeze excess moisture from potato. Combine potato and egg in medium bowl; divide into eight portions. Cook rösti portions on heated oiled flat plate, flattening with spatula, until browned both sides. Drain on absorbent paper.
4 Slice veal thickly; serve with rösti and remaining salsa verde.
salsa verde Place ingredients in medium bowl; toss gently.

GRILLED LAMB WITH BROAD BEAN AND BEETROOT SALAD

prep & cook time **30 minutes** serves **4**
nutritional count per serving **27.6g total fat (9.4g saturated fat); 2082kJ (498 cal); 12g carbohydrate; 47.5g protein; 6.5g fibre**

2 cups (300g) frozen broad beans
450g can baby beetroots, drained, quartered
60g rocket leaves
4 lamb backstraps (800g)

grilled lamb with broad bean and beetroot salad

anchovy dressing

6 drained anchovy fillets, chopped finely
1 tablespoon rinsed, drained baby capers, chopped finely
2 tablespoons olive oil
2 teaspoons finely grated lemon rind
1 teaspoon dijon mustard
1 tablespoon red wine vinegar

1 Boil, steam or microwave beans until tender; drain. When cool enough to handle, peel away grey-coloured outer shells; place beans in large bowl with beetroot and rocket.
2 Meanwhile, make anchovy dressing. Add 2 tablespoons of the dressing to bowl with salad; toss gently.
3 Cook lamb on heated oiled grill plate (or grill or barbecue), uncovered, brushing occasionally with remaining dressing, until cooked as desired. Slice lamb; serve with salad.
anchovy dressing Combine ingredients in small bowl.

pork red curry with green apple

PORK RED CURRY WITH GREEN APPLE

prep & cook time **35 minutes** serves **4**
nutritional count per serving **52.3g total fat (23.5g saturated fat); 3085kJ (719 cal); 18.5g carbohydrate; 41.4g protein; 7.3g fibre**

¼ cup (60ml) peanut oil
600g pork fillets
¼ cup (75g) red curry paste
1 medium brown onion (150g), chopped coarsely
4cm piece fresh ginger (20g), grated
400ml can coconut milk
⅔ cup (160ml) chicken stock
3 medium green apples (450g)
½ cup (70g) roasted unsalted peanuts
½ cup coarsely chopped fresh thai basil

1 Heat half the oil in large saucepan; cook pork, uncovered, until browned. Remove from pan; cover to keep warm.
2 Heat remaining oil in same cleaned pan; cook paste, onion and ginger, stirring, until onion softens. Add coconut milk and stock; bring to the boil. Reduce heat; simmer, uncovered, 5 minutes.
3 Meanwhile, peel, core and thinly slice apples. Return pork to pan with apple; simmer, covered, about 10 minutes or until apple softens. Remove from heat; remove pork, slice thickly.
4 Divide pork among bowls; top with curry mixture then sprinkle with nuts and basil.

PORK, ROCKET AND SOPRESSA PASTA

prep & cook time **35 minutes** serves **4**
nutritional count per serving **27.8g total fat (6.4g saturated fat); 3047kJ (729 cal); 67.2g carbohydrate; 50.1g protein; 4.1g fibre**

100g baby rocket leaves
¼ cup (60ml) olive oil
2 tablespoons lemon juice
375g fettuccine pasta
600g pork fillets
1 medium brown onion (150g), chopped finely
1 clove garlic, crushed
100g hot sopressa, sliced thinly

1 Blend or process rocket, oil and juice until rocket is finely chopped.
2 Cook pasta in large saucepan of boiling water until tender; drain.
3 Meanwhile, cook pork, uncovered, in heated oiled large frying pan, until cooked as desired. Remove from pan; cover to keep warm.
4 Cook onion, garlic and sopressa in same pan, stirring, until onion softens.
5 Thinly slice pork; combine pasta in large bowl with pork and rocket and sopressa mixtures.
note **Sopressa, a salami from the north of Italy, can be found in both mild and chilli-flavoured varieties. If you can't find it easily, you can use any hot salami, but the taste won't be exactly the same.**

pork, rocket and sopressa pasta

LAMB RACKS WITH MUSTARD MAPLE GLAZE

prep & cook time **30 minutes** serves **4**
nutritional count per serving **26.2g total fat (13.8g saturated fat); 2153kJ (515 cal); 44.4g carbohydrate; 22.8g protein; 5.5g fibre**

4 x 4 french-trimmed lamb cutlet racks (720g)
2 cloves garlic, sliced thinly
2 medium parsnips (500g), cut into 2cm cubes
2 small kumara (500g), cut into 2cm cubes
½ cup loosely packed fresh flat-leaf parsley leaves

mustard maple glaze

50g butter
⅓ cup (80ml) maple syrup
2 tablespoons wholegrain mustard

1 Preheat oven to 200°C/180°C fan-forced.
2 Make mustard maple glaze.
3 Meanwhile, using sharp knife, make cuts in lamb; press garlic slices into cuts. Place lamb in large oiled baking dish; brush with 2 tablespoons of the glaze.
4 Combine remaining glaze, parsnip and kumara in medium bowl.
5 Place vegetables in baking dish with lamb; roast, uncovered, about 15 minutes or until vegetables are tender and lamb is cooked as desired. Stir parsley into vegetables; serve with lamb.

mustard maple glaze Combine ingredients in small saucepan; cook, stirring, until glaze is thickened slightly.

LAMB WITH PECAN TOMATO SALSA

prep & cook time **15 minutes** serves **4**
nutritional count per serving **49.5g total fat (10.7g saturated fat); 2721kJ (651 cal); 4.6g carbohydrate; 46.1g protein; 4.2g fibre**

To make salsa, combine 2 tablespoons each olive oil and balsamic vinegar, 1 crushed garlic clove, 2 teaspoons grated lemon rind, 1 cup chopped roasted pecans, 2 chopped seeded small tomatoes, 1 chopped medium red onion and ½ cup chopped fresh flat-leaf parsley in medium bowl. Cook 800g lamb backstraps on heated oiled grill plate (or grill or barbecue) until cooked as desired. Cover; stand 5 minutes then slice thickly. Top salsa with lamb.
serve with **steamed basmati rice.**

PEPPERONI PIZZETTA

prep & cook time **15 minutes** serves **4**
nutritional count per serving **25.4g total fat (9.9g saturated fat); 2592kJ (620 cal); 65.5g carbohydrate; 29g protein; 6.2g fibre**

Preheat oven to 220°C/200°C fan-forced. Place four small pizza bases on oven trays. Spread bases with ⅔ cup tomato paste; top with 160g thinly sliced pepperoni then sprinkle with two thinly sliced fresh small red thai chillies. Bake about 8 minutes. Combine 1 cup flaked parmesan cheese, 60g baby rocket leaves and 2 tablespoons lemon juice in small bowl. Serve pizzettas topped with rocket salad.

15-MINUTE MEALS

HERB-CRUMBED BEEF FILLETS

prep & cook time **15 minutes** serves **4**
nutritional count per serving **21g total fat (10.5g saturated fat); 1768kJ (423 cal); 13.1g carbohydrate; 45.1g protein; 0.9g fibre**

Cook four 200g beef scotch fillet steaks, uncovered, in heated oiled large frying pan until cooked as desired; place on oven tray. Combine 1¼ cups fresh breadcrumbs, 40g melted butter, 1 tablespoon wholegrain mustard, 1 tablespoon finely chopped fresh basil and 2 teaspoons finely chopped fresh rosemary in small bowl. Sprinkle breadcrumb mixture over top of steaks; brown lightly under preheated grill.
serve with **chunky potato chips or mashed potatoes.**

PLUM AND SOY WOK-FRIED PORK

prep & cook time **15 minutes** serves **4**
nutritional count per serving **13.2g total fat (2.9g saturated fat); 1668kJ (399 cal); 30.4g carbohydrate; 37.7g protein; 3.3g fibre**

Heat 1 tablespoon peanut oil in wok; stir-fry 600g thinly sliced pork fillets, in batches, until browned. Remove from wok. Heat another tablespoon peanut oil in wok; stir-fry 1 thickly sliced large brown onion and 1 crushed garlic clove 1 minute. Add 340g trimmed asparagus and 2 sliced medium red capsicums; stir-fry until softened. Return pork to wok with combined ½ cup plum sauce and 2 tablespoons light soy sauce; stir-fry until pork is cooked as desired.
serve with **steamed jasmine rice.**

SPAGHETTI WITH PESTO

prep & cook time 30 minutes **serves** 4
nutritional count per serving 45.2g total fat (8.9g saturated fat); 3578kJ (859 cal); 86.2g carbohydrate; 23.6g protein; 5.6g fibre

2 cloves garlic, chopped coarsely
⅓ cup (50g) roasted pine nuts
½ cup (40g) finely grated parmesan cheese
2 cups firmly packed fresh basil leaves
½ cup (125ml) olive oil
500g spaghetti
½ cup (40g) flaked parmesan cheese

1 Blend or process garlic, nuts, grated cheese and basil until almost smooth. Gradually add oil in a thin, steady stream, processing until thick.
2 Cook pasta in large saucepan of boiling water until just tender; drain, reserving ¼ cup of the cooking liquid.
3 Combine pasta, pesto and reserved cooking liquid in large bowl. Serve with flaked cheese.

EGGS & VEGIES

red curry lentils

RED CURRY LENTILS

prep & cook time **20 minutes** serves **4**
nutritional count per serving **10.5g total fat (2.2g saturated fat); 865kJ (207 cal); 14.3g carbohydrate; 11g protein; 6g fibre**

1 tablespoon olive oil
1 medium brown onion (150g), quartered
2 tablespoons red curry paste
2 x 400g cans brown lentils, rinsed, drained
1 cup (250ml) vegetable stock
200g green beans, halved
2 tablespoons lime juice
⅔ cup (190g) yogurt

1 Heat oil in medium saucepan; cook onion, stirring, until soft. Add paste; cook, stirring, until fragrant. Add lentils and stock; bring to the boil. Reduce heat; simmer, uncovered, about 10 minutes or until stock has thickened. Add beans, simmer 2 minutes. Remove from heat; stir in juice.
2 Divide curry among serving bowls; serve topped with yogurt.

broad bean and ricotta orecchiette

BROAD BEAN AND RICOTTA ORECCHIETTE

prep & cook time **30 minutes** serves **4**
nutritional count per serving **25.2g total fat (13.4g saturated fat); 2500kJ (598 cal); 67.4g carbohydrate; 21.3g protein; 7.9g fibre**

375g orecchiette pasta
1 tablespoon olive oil
2 cups (300g) fresh shelled broad beans
1 clove garlic, crushed
½ cup (125ml) cream
1 teaspoon finely grated lemon rind
2 tablespoons lemon juice
200g ricotta cheese, crumbled
½ cup coarsely chopped fresh mint

1 Cook pasta in large saucepan of boiling water until tender; drain.
2 Meanwhile, heat oil in large frying pan; cook beans and garlic until beans are just tender. Add cream, rind and juice; simmer, uncovered, until sauce thickens slightly.
3 Combine pasta, sauce, cheese and mint in large bowl.

SPICED PUMPKIN SOUP WITH CINNAMON CREAM

prep & cook time **30 minutes** serves **4**
nutritional count per serving **23.2g total fat (12.9g saturated fat); 1530kJ (366 cal); 28.6g carbohydrate; 8.8g protein; 4.5g fibre**

1 tablespoon olive oil
1 medium brown onion (150g), chopped coarsely
1 clove garlic, crushed
2 teaspoons ground cumin
½ teaspoon ground coriander
1kg butternut pumpkin, chopped coarsely
2 medium potatoes (400g), chopped coarsely
2 cups (500ml) water
1½ cups (375ml) vegetable stock
5cm strip orange rind

cinnamon cream
⅔ cup (160ml) cream
½ teaspoon ground cinnamon

1 Heat oil in large saucepan; cook onion and garlic, stirring, until onion softens. Add spices; cook, stirring, until fragrant. Add pumpkin, potato, the water, stock and rind; bring to the boil. Reduce heat; simmer, covered, 20 minutes or until vegetables are tender.
2 Meanwhile, make cinnamon cream.
3 Stand soup 10 minutes then blend or process, in batches, until smooth. Return soup to pan; stir over heat until hot.
4 Serve soup topped with cinnamon cream.
cinnamon cream Beat ingredients in small bowl with electric mixer until soft peaks form.

chilli and mint eggplant burgers

CHILLI AND MINT EGGPLANT BURGERS

prep & cook time **30 minutes** serves **4**
nutritional count per serving **23g total fat (6g saturated fat); 2684kJ (642 cal); 77.9g carbohydrate; 24.3g protein; 12.3g fibre**

¼ cup (35g) plain flour
2 eggs
½ cup (85g) polenta
1 teaspoon hot paprika
1 medium eggplant (300g)
vegetable oil, for shallow-frying
1 large loaf turkish bread (430g), quartered
8 large butter lettuce leaves
80g cheddar cheese, cut into 4 slices
½ cup loosely packed fresh mint leaves
⅓ cup (80ml) sweet chilli sauce

1 Place flour in small shallow bowl. Beat eggs in second small shallow bowl. Combine polenta and paprika in third small shallow bowl.
2 Slice eggplant into 8 slices crossways; discard two skin-side pieces. Coat slices, one at a time, in flour, shake away excess, dip in egg then coat in polenta mixture.
3 Heat oil in large frying pan; shallow-fry eggplant, in batches, until browned lightly both sides. Drain on absorbent paper.
4 Meanwhile, preheat grill.
5 Halve each quarter of bread horizontally. Toast cut sides under grill.
6 Sandwich lettuce, eggplant, cheese, sauce and mint between toasted bread quarters.
note **Grill cheese to melt before topping with sauce and mint, if you like.**

POTATO AND BACON PIZZA

prep & cook time **35 minutes** serves **4**
nutritional count per serving **25.7g total fat (7.6g saturated fat); 3486kJ (834 cal); 105.6g carbohydrate; 39.6g protein; 9g fibre**

2 x 335g pizza bases
2 tablespoons olive oil
4 rindless bacon rashers (260g), chopped coarsely
2 cloves garlic, sliced thinly

potato and bacon pizza

1 tablespoon coarsely chopped fresh rosemary
½ teaspoon dried chilli flakes
500g potatoes, sliced thinly
1 cup (80g) finely grated parmesan cheese

1 Preheat oven to 220°C/200°C fan-forced. Place pizza bases on oven trays; bake about 10 minutes or until crisp.
2 Meanwhile, heat oil in large frying pan; cook bacon, garlic, rosemary and chilli, stirring, 5 minutes. Remove mixture from pan.
3 Add potato to same pan; cook, stirring frequently, about 10 minutes or until tender.
4 Sprinkle each pizza base with ⅓ cup of the cheese. Divide bacon mixture and potato over bases; top with remaining cheese. Bake, in oven, about 5 minutes.

tofu, cashew and vegie stir-fry

TOFU, CASHEW AND VEGIE STIR-FRY

prep & cook time **15 minutes** serves **4**

nutritional count per serving **22.6g total fat (3.4g saturated fat); 1563kJ (374 cal); 20.9g carbohydrate; 18.2g protein; 8.4g fibre**

1 tablespoon vegetable oil
1 fresh long red chilli, sliced thinly
500g packaged fresh stir-fry vegetables
400g packaged marinated tofu pieces, chopped coarsely
½ cup (75g) roasted unsalted cashews
⅓ cup (80ml) hoisin sauce
1 tablespoon lime juice

1 Heat oil in wok; stir-fry chilli, vegetables, tofu and nuts until vegetables are just tender.
2 Add sauce and juice; stir-fry until hot.

SPINACH AND BEETROOT TART

prep & cook time **30 minutes** serves **4**

nutritional count per serving **21.4g total fat (12.8g saturated fat); 1421kJ (340 cal); 22.1g carbohydrate; 13.4g protein; 4g fibre**

1 sheet ready-rolled puff pasty
250g frozen spinach, thawed, drained
1 cup (200g) crumbled fetta cheese,
½ x 850g can drained baby beetroot, sliced thinly

1 Preheat oven to 220°C/200°C fan-forced.
2 Place pastry on oiled oven tray. Fold edges of pastry over to make a 0.5cm border all the way around pastry. Prick pastry base with fork. Place another oven tray on top of pastry; bake 10 minutes. Remove top tray from pastry; reduce temperature to 200°C/180°C fan-forced.
3 Meanwhile, combine spinach with half the cheese in medium bowl.
4 Top tart with spinach mixture, beetroot and remaining cheese. Bake about 10 minutes.

spinach and beetroot tart

spanish cheese and tomato tortilla

SPANISH CHEESE AND TOMATO TORTILLA

prep & cook time **35 minutes** serves **4**
nutritional count per serving **49.9g total fat (29g saturated fat); 2424kJ (580 cal); 7.6g carbohydrate; 25.6g protein; 2.2g fibre**

4 green onions, sliced thickly
1 medium red capsicum (200g), chopped coarsely
2 cloves garlic, crushed
1 fresh long red chilli, chopped finely
2 medium tomatoes (300g), chopped coarsely
200g fetta cheese, crumbled
8 eggs
300ml cream
¼ cup firmly packed fresh flat-leaf parsley leaves, chopped coarsely

1 Heat oiled 26cm-base frying pan; cook onion, capsicum, garlic and chilli, stirring, until vegetables are just tender. Remove from heat; stir in tomato and cheese.
2 Whisk eggs, cream and parsley in large jug; pour over capsicum mixture, stir gently.
3 Return pan to low heat; cook tortilla, uncovered, until just set.
4 Meanwhile, preheat grill.
5 Place pan under grill to brown tortilla top (protect handle with foil, if necessary). Cut into wedges to serve.
serve with **a green salad.**

spaghetti carbonara with peas

SPAGHETTI CARBONARA WITH PEAS

prep & cook time **25 minutes** serves **4**
nutritional count per serving **15.3g total fat (6.3g saturated fat); 2332kJ (558 cal); 66.8g carbohydrate; 35g protein; 5.1g fibre**

4 egg yolks
¾ cup (60g) finely grated parmesan cheese
4 rindless bacon rashers (260g), chopped finely
2 cloves garlic, sliced thinly
1 cup (120g) frozen peas
375g spaghetti

1 Combine egg yolks and cheese in small bowl.
2 Cook bacon over heat in medium frying pan about 5 minutes or until starting to crisp. Add garlic; cook, stirring, 1 minute. Add peas; cook, stirring, until heated through.
3 Meanwhile, cook pasta in large saucepan of boiling water until tender; drain, reserving ¼ cup cooking liquid.
4 Return pasta to saucepan. Add bacon mixture, egg mixture and reserved cooking liquid to pasta; stir over heat about 1 minute.
5 Accompany with extra parmesan cheese, if you like.

NOODLES AND BUK CHOY WITH MIXED GARLIC MUSHROOMS

prep & cook time **30 minutes** serves **4**
nutritional count per serving **11.5g total fat (2g saturated fat); 1033kJ (247 cal); 84.5g carbohydrate; 20.3g protein; 9.2g fibre**

600g fresh thin egg noodles
2 tablespoons peanut oil
1 tablespoon finely grated lemon rind
1 teaspoon chilli flakes
2 baby buk choy, leaves separated
¼ cup (60ml) lemon juice
4 cloves garlic, crushed
150g oyster mushrooms, halved
100g fresh shiitake mushrooms, halved
200g swiss brown mushrooms, halved
2 tablespoons kecap manis

1 Place noodles in large heatproof bowl, cover with boiling water; separate with fork, drain.
2 Heat half the oil in wok. Add rind and chilli; stir until fragrant. Add noodles, buk choy and juice; stir-fry until buk choy wilts. Remove from wok; cover to keep warm.
3 Heat remaining oil in wok; cook garlic, stirring, until fragrant. Add mushrooms and kecap manis; stir-fry until mushrooms soften.
4 Serve mushrooms on noodle mixture.

PIZZETTA CAPRESE

prep & cook time **15 minutes** serves **4**
nutritional count per serving **9g total fat (3.6g saturated fat); 1693kJ (405 cal); 61.3g carbohydrate; 16.3g protein; 5.6g fibre**

Preheat oven to 220°C/200°C fan-forced. Place four small pizza bases on oven trays. Thinly slice 8 cherry bocconcini cheeses. Place cheese and 2 thinly sliced garlic cloves on bases. Bake about 8 minutes. Serve pizzettas topped with 4 thinly sliced small tomatoes and ⅓ cup loosely packed fresh basil leaves.

FETTA AND ARTICHOKE PIZZETTA

prep & cook time **15 minutes** serves **4**
nutritional count per serving **22g total fat (9.2g saturated fat); 2223kJ (532 cal); 60.8g carbohydrate; 20.3g protein; 4.2g fibre**

Preheat oven to 220°C/200°C fan-forced. Place four small pizza bases on oven trays. Combine 50g soft fetta cheese with 1 tablespoon olive oil. Spread pizza bases with cheese paste; top with 4 thinly sliced marinated artichokes then sprinkle with another 150g crumbled soft fetta cheese. Bake about 8 minutes. Serve pizzettas sprinkled with ⅓ cup loosely packed fresh oregano leaves and 2 tablespoons lime juice.

15-MINUTE MEALS

LEMON, PEA AND RICOTTA PASTA

prep & cook time **15 minutes** serves **4**
nutritional count per serving **15.6g total fat (4.7g saturated fat); 2123kJ (508 cal); 69g carbohydrate; 19g protein; 6.9g fibre**

Cook 375g angel hair pasta in large saucepan of boiling water until tender; add 2 cups frozen peas during last minute of pasta cooking time. Drain, reserving ¼ cup cooking liquid. Rinse pasta and peas under cold water; drain. Meanwhile, heat 2 tablespoons olive oil in small frying pan; cook 2 thinly sliced garlic cloves, stirring, until fragrant. Combine pasta and peas in large bowl with reserved cooking liquid, garlic mixture, 2 teaspoons finely grated lemon rind and ½ cup lemon juice; stir in 180g crumbled ricotta cheese.

EGG SALAD WITH CROÛTONS

prep & cook time **15 minutes** serves **4**
nutritional count per serving **18.1g total fat (4.1g saturated fat); 1099kJ (263 cal); 13.2g carbohydrate; 10g protein; 4.2g fibre**

Separate leaves of one medium butter lettuce. Divide lettuce, 250g halved cherry tomatoes, 2 thinly sliced shallots and ⅓ cup ranch dressing among four serving bowls. Serve topped with 4 halved hard-boiled eggs and 75g packet croûtons.

PERFECT MASHED POTATO

prep & cook time **30 minutes** serves **4**
nutritional count per serving **10.2g total fat (6.6g saturated fat); 1028kJ (246 cal); 30.1g carbohydrate; 6.7g protein; 3.4g fibre**

Boil, steam or microwave 1kg coarsely chopped potatoes until tender; drain. Using the back of a wooden spoon, push potato through fine sieve into large bowl. Stir in 40g butter and ¾ cup hot milk.

note **Using hot milk gives a creamier mash.**

ORANGE MAPLE BABY CARROTS

prep & cook time **30 minutes** serves **4**
nutritional count per serving **3.3g total fat (2g saturated fat); 426kJ (102 cal); 14.2g carbohydrate; 1.4g protein; 5.1g fibre**

Boil, steam or microwave 800g baby carrots until just tender. Melt 15g butter in large frying pan; stir 1 teaspoon finely grated orange rind, 1 tablespoon orange juice and 1 tablespoon maple syrup in pan until mixture boils. Reduce heat; simmer, uncovered, until syrup mixture thickens slightly. Add drained carrots to pan; stir gently to coat in orange maple syrup.

GREEN BEANS ALMONDINE

prep & cook time **15 minutes** serves **4**
nutritional count per serving **11.5g total fat (3.9g saturated fat); 602kJ (144 cal); 2.3g carbohydrate; 6.9g protein; 2.9g fibre**

Cook 300g green beans until just tender; drain. Rinse beans under cold water; drain. Melt 20g butter in large frying pan; cook 1 crushed garlic clove, 1 finely chopped rindless bacon rasher and ¼ cup slivered almonds, stirring, until bacon crisps. Add beans; stir until hot.

CELERIAC PUREE

prep & cook time **35 minutes** serves **4**
nutritional count per serving **14.4g total fat (9.2g saturated fat); 815kJ (195 cal); 7.4g carbohydrate; 5.2g protein; 8.8g fibre**

Peel and coarsely chop 1kg celeriac. Bring 2 cups chicken stock to the boil in medium saucepan; add celeriac, return to the boil. Reduce heat; simmer, covered, about 30 minutes or until celeriac is tender. Drain. Stand 10 minutes then blend or process celeriac, in batches, with ½ cup cream until smooth. Serve sprinkled with 1 tablespoon finely chopped fresh chives.

SIDES

SOY DRESSED ASIAN GREENS

prep & cook time **15 minutes** serves **4**
nutritional count per serving **1g total fat (0.1g saturated fat); 150kJ (36 cal); 2.5g carbohydrate; 2.9g protein; 2.8g fibre**

Combine 2cm piece finely chopped fresh ginger, 2 tablespoons rice vinegar, 2 tablespoons light soy sauce and ½ teaspoon sesame oil in bowl. Cook 350g trimmed gai lan and 500g trimmed and quartered baby buk choy, separately, until tender; drain. Drizzle dressing over asian greens to serve.

STEAMED JASMINE RICE

prep & cook time **20 minutes** serves **4**
nutritional count per serving **0.3g total fat (0g saturated fat); 752kJ (180 cal); 39.9g carbohydrate; 3.3g protein; 1.1g fibre**

Rinse 1 cup jasmine rice under cold water until water runs clear; drain. Bring 2 cups water to the boil, covered, in medium saucepan; add rice. Cook, covered, over low heat, 10 minutes. Remove from heat; stand, covered, 10 minutes. Fluff rice with fork.

CREAMED SPINACH

prep & cook time **15 minutes** serves **4**
nutritional count per serving **38.7g total fat (25.4g saturated fat); 1555kJ (372 cal); 2.8g carbohydrate; 3.5g protein; 2.1g fibre**

Melt 20g butter in large frying pan; cook 600g trimmed spinach, stirring, until wilted. Add ½ cup cream; bring to the boil. Reduce heat; simmer, uncovered, until liquid reduces by half.

PERFECT ROAST POTATOES

prep & cook time **35 minutes** serves **4**
nutritional count per serving **9.4g total fat (1.3g saturated fat); 1247kJ (298 cal); 42.5g carbohydrate; 7.8g protein; 5.2g fibre**

Pour 2 tablespoons oil into a shallow-sided oven tray; put tray into cold oven. Preheat oven to the hottest setting possible. Peel and halve 6 medium pontiac potatoes lengthways. Boil, steam or microwave potato until cooked through; drain. Dry potatoes thoroughly then roughly score the outside with a fork. Once the oven has reached its hottest temperature, remove oven tray and place potatoes on tray; return tray with potatoes to oven then reduce oven temperature to 200°C/180°C fan-forced. Cook potatoes 25 minutes or until golden brown.

ARBORIO RICE a small round-rice grain well suited to absorb a large amount of liquid; a good rice to use in risottos.

BACON, SHORTCUT is a "half rasher"; the streaky narrow portion of the rasher (belly) has been removed leaving the choice cut eye meat (fat end).

BEANS

broad also known as fava, windsor and horse beans. Fresh and frozen beans should be peeled twice, discarding the outer long green pod and the beige-green tough inner shell.

four-bean mix is a mix of kidney, butter and cannellini beans and chickpeas.

sprouts also known as bean shoots; tender new growths of beans and seeds germinated for consumption as sprouts.

white in this book, some recipes may simply call for "white beans", a generic term we use for canned or dried cannellini, haricot, navy or great northern beans of which any can be used.

BEAN THREAD NOODLES made from extruded mung bean paste; also known as wun sen or cellophane or glass noodles because they are transparent when cooked.

BEETROOT also known as red beets or just beets; firm, round root vegetable.

BREAD

lavash (lavosh) flat, unleavened bread of Mediterranean origin.

mountain bread a thin, dry, soft-textured bread that can be used for sandwiches or rolled up and filled with your favourite filling.

tortillas thin, round unleavened bread originating in Mexico. Two kinds are available, one made from wheat flour and the other from corn.

BUCKWHEAT not a cereal so is gluten-free. Available as flour; ground (cracked) into coarse, medium or fine grain; or as groats, the roasted whole kernels cooked similarly to rice or couscous.

BURGHUL also bulgar or bulghur; a form of whole wheat that has been cleaned, parboiled or steamed, dried and ground into grains of several distinct sizes.

BUTTERMILK originally the term given to the slightly sour liquid left after butter was churned from cream, today it is made similarly to yogurt. Sold alongside all fresh milk products in supermarkets. Despite the implication of its name, it is low in fat.

BUTTERNUT PUMPKIN (squash) pear-shaped with a golden skin and orange flesh.

CAPERS the grey-green buds of a warm climate shrub (usually Mediterranean), sold either dried and salted or pickled in a vinegar brine. Baby capers are very small and fuller-flavoured than the full-size ones. They must be rinsed well before using.

CAPSICUM also known as bell pepper or, simply, pepper. The seeds and membranes should be discarded before use.

CAYENNE PEPPER a long, thin-fleshed, extremely hot red chilli usually sold dried and ground.

CHEESE

cottage a fresh, grainy, white, unripened curd cheese.

fetta salty white crumbly cheese with a milky, fresh acidity; made with goat's- or sheep's-milk.

mozzarella a soft, spun-curd cheese. It has a low melting point and a wonderfully elastic texture when heated; is used to add texture rather than flavour.

parmesan also known as parmigiano; a hard, grainy cow's-milk cheese. The curd is salted in brine for a month before being aged for up to two years.

ricotta a low-fat, fresh unripened cheese made from whey; is a sweet, moist cheese with a slightly grainy texture.

CHICKPEAS also called channa, garbanzos or hummus; a round, sandy-coloured legume.

CHILLI available in many different types and sizes. Use rubber gloves when seeding and chopping fresh chillies as they can burn your skin. Removing seeds and membranes lessens the heat level.

flakes deep-red, dehydrated, fine slices and whole seeds.

long red available both fresh and dried; a generic term used for any moderately hot, long (6cm-8cm) thin chilli.

thai red small, hot and bright red in colour.

CORIANDER also known as pak chee, cilantro or chinese parsley; bright-green leafy herb with a pungent flavour. The stems and roots are used in Thai cooking; wash well before using. Also available ground or as seeds; these should not be substituted for fresh coriander as the tastes are completely different.

GLOSSARY

CORNFLOUR also known as cornstarch; used as a thickening agent. Available as 100% maize (corn) and wheaten cornflour (which has some gluten).

CUMIN a spice also known as zeera or comino; has a spicy, nutty flavour.

EGGPLANT (aubergine) a purple-skinned vegetable.

FENNEL BULB also known as finocchio or anise; a white to very pale green, firm, crisp, roundish vegetable about 8cm-12cm in diameter. The bulb has a slightly sweet, anise flavour but the leaves have a much stronger taste.

FIRM WHITE FISH FILLET blue eye, bream, flathead, swordfish, ling, whiting, jewfish, snapper or sea perch are all good choices. Check for small bones and use tweezers to remove them.

FLOUR

plain an all-purpose flour made from wheat.

self-raising plain flour sifted with baking powder in the proportion of 1 cup flour to 2 teaspoons baking powder.

wholemeal contains the whole wheat grain (bran, germ and flour).

FRÛCHE brand name of a light, fresh French cheese (fromage frais); it has the consistency of thick yogurt with a refreshing, slightly tart taste and a smooth, creamy texture, yet is low in fat.

GINGER also known as green or root ginger; the thick root of a tropical plant.

ground also known as powdered ginger; used as a flavouring in cakes and puddings, but cannot be substituted for fresh ginger.

JAM also known as conserve.

KECAP MANIS *see sauces*

KIWIFRUIT also known as chinese gooseberry. Has a brown, somewhat hairy skin and bright-green or yellow flesh with a unique sweet-tart flavour.

LEBANESE CUCUMBER short, slender and thin-skinned. Probably the most popular variety because of its tender, edible skin, tiny, yielding seeds, and sweet, fresh and flavoursome taste.

LEMON GRASS a tall, clumping, lemon-smelling and tasting, sharp-edged grass; the white lower part of each stem is chopped and used in cooking.

MARINARA MIX a mixture of fresh uncooked, chopped seafood available from fishmarkets and fishmongers.

MESCLUN mixed baby salad leaves also sold as salad mix or gourmet salad mix.

MINCE known as ground meat.

MIRIN a Japanese champagne-coloured cooking wine; made of glutinous rice and alcohol and used only for cooking. Should not be confused with sake.

ONIONS

green also known as scallion or, incorrectly, shallot; an immature onion picked before the bulb has formed, having a long, bright-green edible stalk.

red also known as red spanish, spanish or bermuda onion; a sweet-flavoured, large, purple-red onion.

PAPRIKA ground dried sweet red capsicum (bell pepper); there are many types available, including sweet, hot, mild and smoked.

PARSLEY, FLAT-LEAF also known as continental parsley or italian parsley.

PEARL BARLEY a nutritious grain used in soups and stews as well as in whisky- and beer-making. Pearl barley has had the husk discarded and been hulled and polished, much the same as rice.

POTATOES

baby new also known as chats; not a separate variety but an early harvest with very thin skin. Can be eaten unpeeled.

kipfler small, finger-shaped potato having a nutty flavour.

PRAWNS also known as shrimp.

RICE PAPER SHEETS also known as banh trang. Made from rice paste and stamped into rounds; stores well at room temperature. Are quite brittle and will break if dropped. Dipped momentarily in water they become pliable wrappers for fried food and uncooked vegetables. They make good spring-roll wrappers.

ROCKET also known as arugula, rugula and rucola. Baby rocket leaves (wild rocket) are both smaller and less peppery.

SAUCES

cranberry made of cranberries cooked in sugar syrup; has an astringent flavour that goes well with roast poultry and meats.

fish also called nam pla or nuoc nam; made from pulverised salted fermented fish, most often anchovies. Has a pungent smell and strong taste, so use sparingly.

hoisin a thick, sweet and spicy Chinese paste made from salted fermented soya beans, onions and garlic; used as a marinade.

soy made from fermented soya beans. Several variations are available in most supermarkets and Asian food stores. We use a mild Japanese variety in our recipes, possibly the best table soy and the one to choose if you only want one variety.

kecap manis a dark, thick, sweet soy sauce. Depending on the brand, the soy's sweetness is derived from the addition of either molasses or palm sugar when brewed.

light fairly thin in consistency and, while paler than the others, is the saltiest tasting; used in dishes where the natural colour of the ingredients is to be maintained. Not to be confused with salt-reduced or low-sodium soy sauces.

sweet chilli a comparatively mild, Thai-style sauce made from red chillies, sugar, garlic and vinegar.

teriyaki a Japanese sauce, made from soy sauce, mirin, sugar, ginger and other spices, imparts a distinctive glaze when brushed over grilled meat.

tomato pasta made from a blend of tomatoes, herbs and spices.

SNOW PEA SPROUTS tender new growths of snow peas; also known as "mange tout".

tendrils are the plant's shoots.

SPINACH also known as english spinach and, incorrectly, silver beet.

SPLIT PEAS a variety of yellow or green pea grown specifically for drying. When dried, the peas usually split along a natural seam. Available, whole or split, in bulk in health-food stores or packaged in supermarkets.

STAR ANISE dried star-shaped pod having an astringent aniseed flavour; used to favour stocks and marinades. Available whole and ground, it is an essential ingredient in five-spice powder.

STARFRUIT also known as carambola, five-corner fruit or chinese starfruit; pale green or yellow in colour. Has a clean, crisp texture; flavour may be either sweet or sour, depending on the variety and when picked. No need to be peeled or seeded. Are slow to discolour; avoid ones with brown spots or streaks.

SUGAR

brown an extremely soft, finely granulated sugar retaining molasses for its characteristic colour and flavour.

caster also known as superfine or finely granulated table sugar.

icing sugar also known as confectioners' sugar or powdered sugar; granulated sugar crushed together with a small amount of added cornflour.

white a coarse, granulated table sugar, also known as crystal sugar.

VINEGAR

balsamic made from the juice of Trebbiano grapes; is a deep rich brown colour with a sweet and sour flavour.

balsamic white condiment is a clear and lighter version of balsamic vinegar; it has a fresh, sweet clean taste.

cider (apple cider) made from fermented apples.

raspberry fresh raspberries are steeped in a white wine vinegar.

red wine based on fermented red wine.

white wine made from a blend of white wines.

WATER CHESTNUTS resembles a chestnut in appearance, hence the English name. They are small brown tubers with a crisp, white, nutty-tasting flesh. Their crunchy texture is best experienced fresh, however, canned water chestnuts are more easily obtained and can be kept about a month, once opened, under refrigeration.

WATERCRESS also known as winter rocket. Is one of the cress family, a large group of peppery greens. Highly perishable, so must be used as soon as possible after purchase.

WHEATGERM usually separated from the bran and starch during the milling of flour because the germ's perishable oil content limits the keeping time of the flour. It is available from health-food stores and supermarkets.

WOMBOK also known as peking cabbage, chinese cabbage or petsai. Elongated in shape with pale green, crinkly leaves, this is the most common cabbage in South-East Asian cooking.

WONTON WRAPPERS also known as wonton skins; made from flour, eggs and water, and come in varying thicknesses and shapes (round or square). Sold packaged in large amounts and found in the refrigerated section of Asian grocery stores and larger supermarkets; gow gee, egg or spring roll pastry sheets can be substituted.

ZUCCHINI (courgette); small green, yellow or white vegetable belonging to the squash family.

CONVERSION CHART

MEASURES

One Australian metric measuring cup holds approximately 250ml, one Australian metric tablespoon holds 20ml, one Australian metric teaspoon holds 5ml.

The difference between one country's measuring cups and another's is within a 2- or 3-teaspoon variance, and will not affect your cooking results. North America, New Zealand and the United Kingdom use a 15ml tablespoon. All cup and spoon measurements are level. The most accurate way of measuring dry ingredients is to weigh them. When measuring liquids, use a clear glass or plastic jug with metric markings.

We use large eggs with an average weight of 60g.

DRY MEASURES

METRIC	IMPERIAL
15g	½oz
30g	1oz
60g	2oz
90g	3oz
125g	4oz (¼lb)
155g	5oz
185g	6oz
220g	7oz
250g	8oz (½lb)
280g	9oz
315g	10oz
345g	11oz
375g	12oz (¾lb)
410g	13oz
440g	14oz
470g	15oz
500g	16oz (1lb)
750g	24oz (1½lb)
1kg	32oz (2lb)

LIQUID MEASURES

METRIC	IMPERIAL
30ml	1 fluid oz
60ml	2 fluid oz
100ml	3 fluid oz
125ml	4 fluid oz
150ml	5 fluid oz (¼ pint/1 gill)
190ml	6 fluid oz
250ml	8 fluid oz
300ml	10 fluid oz (½ pint)
500ml	16 fluid oz
600ml	20 fluid oz (1 pint)
1000ml (1 litre)	1¾ pints

LENGTH MEASURES

METRIC	IMPERIAL
3mm	⅛in
6mm	¼in
1cm	½in
2cm	¾in
2.5cm	1in
5cm	2in
6cm	2½in
8cm	3in
10cm	4in
13cm	5in
15cm	6in
18cm	7in
20cm	8in
23cm	9in
25cm	10in
28cm	11in
30cm	12in (1ft)

OVEN TEMPERATURES

These oven temperatures are only a guide for conventional ovens. For fan-forced ovens, check the manufacturer's manual.

	°C (CELSIUS)	°F (FAHRENHEIT)	GAS MARK
Very slow	120	250	½
Slow	150	275-300	1-2
Moderately slow	160	325	3
Moderate	180	350-375	4-5
Moderately hot	200	400	6
Hot	220	425-450	7-8
Very hot	240	475	9

INDEX

ACP BOOKS
General manager Christine Whiston
Editor-in-chief Susan Tomnay
Creative director Hieu Chi Nguyen
Art director & designer Hannah Blackmore
Senior editor Wendy Bryant
Food director Pamela Clark
Food editor + nutritional information Rebecca Squadrito
Sales & rights director Brian Cearnes
Marketing manager Bridget Cody
Senior business analyst Rebecca Varela
Circulation manager Jarna Mclean
Operations manager David Scotto
Production manager Victoria Jefferys

ACP Books are published by ACP Magazines
a division of PBL Media Pty Limited
PBL Media, Chief Executive officer Ian Law
Publishing & sales director, Women's lifestyle Lynette Phillips
General manager, Editorial projects, Women's lifestyle Deborah Thomas
Group editorial director, Women's lifestyle Pat Ingram
Marketing director, Women's lifestyle Matthew Dominello
Commercial manager, Women's lifestyle Seymour Cohen
Research Director, Women's lifestyle Justin Stone

Produced by ACP Books, Sydney.

Published by ACP Books, a division of ACP Magazines Ltd, 54 Park St, Sydney; GPO Box 4088, Sydney, NSW 2001.
phone (02) 9282 8618; fax (02) 9267 9438. acpbooks@acpmagazines.com.au; www.acpbooks.com.au

Printed by Toppan Printing Co., China.

Australia Distributed by Network Services, phone +61 2 9282 8777;
fax +61 2 9264 3278; networkweb@networkservicescompany.com.au
United Kingdom Distributed by Australian Consolidated Press (UK), phone (01604) 642 200;
fax (01604) 642 300; books@acpuk.com
New Zealand Distributed by Netlink Distribution Company, phone (9) 366 9966; ask@ndc.co.nz
South Africa Distributed by PSD Promotions, phone (27 11) 392 6065/6/7;
fax (27 11) 392 6079/80; orders@psdprom.co.za
Canada Distributed by Publishers Group Canada
phone (800) 663 5714; fax (800) 565 3770; service@raincoast.com

Midweek meals / food director Pamela Clark.
ISBN: 978 1 86396 9 284 (pbk.)
Notes: Includes index.
Subjects: Cookery.
Other Authors/Contributors: Clark, Pamela.
Dewey Number: 641.5

ABN 18 053 273 546

Cover Honeyed ginger fish bundles, page 7
Photographer Ian Wallace
Stylist Louise Pickford
Food preparation Rebecca Squadrito

Send recipe enquiries to: recipeenquiries@acpmagazines.com.au